SIMPLE
PLEASURES
Tea

CONARI PRESS

First published in 2004 by Conari Press,
an imprint of Red Wheel/Weiser, LLC
York Beach, ME
With offices at:
368 Congress Street
Boston, MA 02210
www.redwheelweiser.com

Adapted from the *Simple Pleasures* series by Susannah Seton first published in
1996 by Conari Press.
Recipe on page 31 adapted from Romancing the Stove by Margie Lapanja first
published in 2003 by Conari Press.

ISBN 1-57324-217-9

Printed in China
EV

11 10 09 08 07 06 05 04
   8 7 6 5 4 3 2 1

The paper used in this publication meets the minimum requirements of the
American National Standard for Information Sciences—Permanence of Paper
for Printed Library Materials Z39.48-1992 (R1997).

"Tea, thou soft, thou sober, sage, and venerable drink…"
—Colley Cibber

O n cold winter nights, nothing beats curling up in front of the fireplace with a cup of hot tea and a good book. The mug warms my hands; the delicious liquid warms my insides going down. My personal favorite is Earl Gray. I love that flowery, mysterious flavor—but no milk and sugar for me. I like mine straight. Recently, though, I have been drinking herbal teas—beside the fact that they are caffeine-free, they have all kinds of health benefits. I like to make my own. It's easy—as long as you don't combine different herbs. Just stick to one herb at a time (professionals call them simples). There's something about making the simple and then drinking it later that feels like a bit of a homey ritual to me.

Herbal Tea Infusions for your health can be found on pages eighteen through twenty. Simple Pleasures of Tea offers recipes for a range of teas (herbal and black), along with easy recipes for delicious baked treats to accompany your teatime, alone or with company. There are also ways in here you'd never imagine to use tea—giving your plants a cup of tea for nourishment, for example, and treating yourself to a steaming tea facial. Drink, eat, and pamper yourself to your heart's content.

 low

We lift our tea cup—of course it is of the finest old India or Chinese porcelain (egg shell preferred)—to our lips. Rest—Peace Ambrosia! We are at one with the gods. They of Olympus with nectar and damp clouds have nothing on us with our sparkling fire and tea inspiring and recreating us.
—Alice Foote McDougall

SIMPLE PLEASURES

Sun tea is great because it has a mellower flavor than brewed tea. Drop four teabags in a quart pitcher of water (the pitcher must be glass). Cover to keep out bugs and put the pitcher outside in the full sun. After a couple of hours, when the sun is really hot and you are too, remove the teabags. Add ice and serve.

For a variation, use a peach fruit tea. When the tea is ready, cut up a chilled peach into bite-sized pieces and add to the tea. Serve immediately for a one-of-a-kind refresher.

7

꧁꧂

"Is it so small a thing
to have enjoy'd the sun,
To have lived light in the spring,
To have loved, to have thought, to have done?"
—Matthew Arnold

STUFFED BAKED PEACHES

10 fresh peaches, pitted and halved
1 egg yolk
7 tablespoons butter, softened
1 cup of crushed Amaretto di Saronno cookies

Remove one spoonful of peach flesh from each peach and puree; set aside. Cream 6 tablespoons of butter in a bowl, stirring in egg yolk, peach puree, and crushed cookies until well combined. Fill each peach half with a generously rounded scoop of the mixture.

Place the peach halves, open side up, in a large glass casserole with the remaining tablespoon of butter, and bake in a preheated oven at 375° for 5–7 minutes or until cookie mixture is lightly browned. Serve peaches at room temperature with crème fraîche or ice cream. Serves 10.

TEA

*D*on't throw leftover herbal tea away—use it to water your houseplants. But be sure it is caffeine free; plants like tea as long as it is "unleaded."

❧

Green fingers are the extensions of a verdant heart.
—Russell Page

Summer is the time for this treat.

3 cups rhubarb, sliced
2 cups strawberries, whole or sliced
juice from one lemon
1 stick butter, softened
1 cup granulated sugar
1 cup flour

Preheat oven to 400°. Combine rhubarb, strawberries, and lemon juice in a 9-by-13-inch baking pan. In a medium bowl, combine the butter, sugar, and flour until crumbly and then spread over rhubarb mixture. Bake uncovered for 20 minutes or until crisp is bubbly and top browned. Serves 6.

*F*reeze little slices of lemon or lime into your ice cubes for a pretty and refreshing touch in iced tea or other cold drinks. You can also freeze orange or cranberry juice into ice cubes to add sparkle to lemon-lime soda.

15

❦

"A little of what you fancy does you good."
—Marie Lloyd

LEMON TEA BREAD

Here's a summer treat for those who grow lemon balm.

1 tablespoon finely chopped lemon balm
1 tablespoon finely chopped lemon thyme
¾ cup low fat milk
2 cups flour
¼ teaspoon salt
1½ teaspoons baking powder
6 tablespoons butter, softened
1 cup sugar
2 eggs, beaten
1 tablespoon grated lemon zest
juice of 2 lemons
confectioners' sugar, about ½–¾ cup

Preheat the oven to 325°. Grease a 9-by-5-by-3-inch loaf pan. In a
small saucepan, gently heat the milk with the lemon balm and thyme
until just before it boils. Remove from heat and let steep until cool.

Combine the flour, salt, and baking powder in a medium bowl.
In a large bowl, cream the butter and sugar together until fluffy. Add

the eggs one at a time and beat well. Add the lemon zest, then part of the flour mixture, then some of the milk. Beat well and continue alternating until well combined.

Pour into prepared pan and bake for about 1 hour or until a toothpick inserted into the center comes out clean. While loaf is cooking, place lemon juice in a small bowl with enough confectioners' sugar to make a thick but still pourable glaze. Stir well.

Remove bread from pan and place on a wire rack that has been set over a piece of waxed paper. Pour glaze over top and allow to cool. Makes 1 loaf.

HERBAL TEA INFUSIONS

Start with a handful of a dried herb of your choice (see list following). Place it in a glass jar and put a stainless steel knife into the jar (to keep the glass from cracking). Pour boiling water into the jar and stir. Put a lid on (a plate will do) and let sit until completely cool. Strain and store in the refrigerator. To serve hot, bring to a boil on the stove or in the microwave.

Blueberry Leaves: A very delicious tea said to be beneficial for blood sugar problems and varicose veins.

Dandelion Root: High in iron, manganese, phosphorous, calcium, magnesium, zinc, and potassium. A diuretic, it is reportedly good for the liver by helping the body remove toxins.

Echinacea Root: Native Americans used it to heal wounds. Modern folks swear by it when a cold or flu is coming on since it is said to boost the immune system.

Fennel Seeds and Leaves: Good for the intestinal tract. A natural breath freshener.

Gingerroot: Good for digestion, nausea, and morning sickness. Is also said to aid circulation. Tea with this herb is made differently—simply cut off a slice of the fresh root, pour boiling water over it, and let steep for ten minutes. (You probably will want to add some sweetener like sugar or honey.)

Nettle: Reputed to be good for kidneys and an immune system booster. Is high in many minerals and vitamins including iron, thiamine, and riboflavin.

BUYING HERBAL TEA

Most health food stores carry herbal teas in bags. But if you want to buy herbs in bulk (store in a dry, dark, glass container), you can contact Blessed Herbs (800-489-4372) or Herbs, Etc. (888-694-3727).

If your tastes don't run to herbal teas, try this wonderfully spicy potion instead. This makes enough for a crowd—try it on a cold winter's evening. I make it unsweetened and allow guests to add their own sugar if they want. You can make it with decaf bags if you want to avoid the kick.

4 cups water
4 cups cranberry juice
4 orange pekoe tea bags
¾ teaspoon cinnamon
16 cloves
1 apple, cored, seeded, and cut into 8 slices

Bring water and juice to a boil over medium heat. Place the tea bags in the mixture, cover, and remove from heat. Let steep 10 minutes. Remove the bags. Add the cinnamon. Place 2 cloves in each apple slice and add to tea. Let steep 5 minutes. Pour into mugs, making sure each cup gets 1 apple slice. Serves 8.

"How beautiful it is to do nothing,
and then rest afterward."
—Spanish proverb

Traditional wedding cookies are often served at other festive occasions as well.

½ cup powdered sugar	¼ teaspoon salt
1 cup butter, softened	¾ cup chopped nuts,
1 teaspoon vanilla	optional
2 ¼ cups flour	additional powdered sugar

Cream together the ½ cup sugar, butter, and vanilla in a large bowl. Sift in the flour and salt. Add the nuts, if using. Cover and chill the dough for 2 hours in the refrigerator or 10 minutes in the freezer. Preheat oven to 400°. Roll the dough into 1-inch balls and place on an ungreased cookie sheet. Bake until set, about 10 minutes. While still warm, roll the cookies in powdered sugar. Makes 4 dozen.

❧

Eros, the god of love, emerged to create the earth.
Before, all was silent, bare, and motionless.
Now, all was life, joy, and motion.
        —Early Greek myth

HONEY-SAGE TEA

This tea may not cure your cold or flu, but it sure will make you feel better.

>   2 tablespoons honey
>   juice of 1 lemon
>   1 ounce sage leaves, torn
>   boiling water

Place honey, lemon, and sage in a mug. Pour the water over and stir to dissolve honey. Cover and let sit for at least 5 minutes. Makes 1 mug of tea.

BUTTERMILK BISCUITS

These are sensational right out of the oven with butter, jelly, honey—or even plain!

2 cups all-purpose flour
2 teaspoons baking powder
½ teaspoon baking soda
½ teaspoon salt
¼ cup vegetable shortening, butter, or margarine
¾ cup buttermilk

Preheat oven to 450°. Combine the first 4 ingredients in a medium bowl. Cut in the shortening, butter, or margarine until the mixture resembles coarse crumbs. Stir in buttermilk. With flour-covered hands, knead gently and then roll out on floured surface to ½-inch thickness. Cut with a 2 ½-inch biscuit cutter and place on a lightly greased baking sheet. Bake for 10 to 15 minutes or until golden. Makes 10.

SIMPLE PLEASURES

TROPICAL BACCHUS BREW

¾ cup sugar
1 quart strong orange-spice tea
1 cup orange juice
1 can 7-Up
4 cups vodka
2 cups dark rum

Stir the sugar, tea, orange juice, and 7-Up together in a large punch bowl until the sugar dissolves. Add the vodka, rum, and bitters and stir well. Add the ice. Wedge a mint leaf into the center of each orange slice, and garnish the brew with oranges and cherries.

Makes enough tropical brew to arouse 4 to 6 bacchants and bacchantes to bliss.

"To affect the quality of the day;
that is the art of life."
—Henry David Thoreau

A friend once related the following story to me: My current schedule requires me to get up earlier than my wife and our two-year-old daughter. I may grumble when the alarm goes off, but I relish that hour of solitude. It's not just sitting at the table drinking coffee and reading the paper in silence. Nor is it the beauty of the morning. What I love is seeing the remains of yesterday's activities and dramas: the stuffed animal wrapped in a dishtowel "blanket" on the chair where we left it last night, the last crackling cinders in the fireplace, a little sock lying under the table. It's sort of an archaeology of the living. I see the object and it brings a flood of memories.

STEAMING TEA FACIAL

1 chamomile tea bag
1 peppermint tea bag
3 cups boiling water

Place the tea bags in a large, wide-mouthed bowl or pot. Add boiling water, and allow to cool for 2 minutes. Place a clean towel over your head and the bowl (keep your face at least eight inches away from the surface of the water), and steam for 10 minutes.

RAISIN SCONES

Scones are becoming increasingly popular breakfast items. They're easy to make, and because these are made with oats, they have the added benefit of being good for you.

⅓ cup butter or
  margarine, melted
⅓ cup milk
1 egg, beaten
1½ cups flour
¼ cup sugar

1 tablespoon
  baking powder
¼ teaspoon salt
¼ teaspoon cream of tartar
1¼ cups quick oats
⅓ cup raisins

Combine butter or margarine with milk and egg in a large bowl. Set aside. Sift together flour, sugar, baking powder, salt, and cream of tartar. Add gradually to milk mixture, stirring well. Add oats and raisins and mix well.

Preheat oven to 400°. With flour-coated hands, form the dough into an 8-inch circle on a lightly floured cookie sheet. Cut into 8 wedges. Separate wedges slightly and bake for 12–15 minutes or until lightly browned. Makes 8.

TEA

*I*t's easy to grow and make your own herbal teas, according to the folks at Yamagami's Nursery in Cupertino, California, who write that one way to start is to grow lemon verbena, lemongrass, spearmint, and peppermint. Lemon verbena is easy to grow in full sun to part shade. Prune it frequently to keep it bushy. Widely used in Asian cuisine, lemongrass is a very fragrant clump grass that grows two to three inches tall and likes full sun. Spearmint and peppermint like moist semishady areas; prune them frequently to keep them low, and beware—they can be invasive so you might want to grow them in containers.

You can throw a small handful of any or all of these fresh herbs into black tea before steeping—just be sure to wash them well beforehand. Or you can dry them and experiment with a variety of combinations and additions, including carefully washed rose petals and hips, chamomile buds or leaves, or lemon or orange slices. A good basic caffeine-free recipe is 3 tablespoons dried lemon verbena, 4 tablespoons dried lemongrass, 1 tablespoon dried spearmint, and 1 tablespoon dried peppermint. Simply crumble dried herbs together, steep in 4 cups of boiling water for 5 minutes and strain. Delicious either hot or iced.

These are simply delicious.

½ cup finely chopped roasted almonds
36 whole almonds
1 cup sifted all-purpose flour
½ teaspoon baking powder
¼ teaspoon salt
½ cup butter or margarine
⅓ cup granulated sugar
½ teaspoon almond extract
1 tablespoon gin, vodka, or water
red food coloring (optional)

Preheat oven to 350°, and grease several cookie sheets. Set the 36 whole almonds to the side. Sift flour with baking powder and salt. Thoroughly cream butter and sugar in a large bowl. Stir in all remaining ingredients except whole almonds. Form dough into 36 balls. Place on greased cookie sheets. Press a whole almond in the center of each ball and dot with a bit of red food coloring. Bake for 20 minutes or until lightly browned. Makes about 3 dozen.

*"Come along inside . . .
We'll see if tea and buns can
make the world a better place."*
—The Wind in the Willows

*F*ill the kettle with fresh cold water. Bring to a rolling boil. Scald teapot with hot water. Place 1 rounded teaspoon of loose tea per cup into an infuser inside the pot (or one tea bag per cup). Pour boiling water into teapot. Let steep for three minutes. Remove tea infuser and serve.

42

❦

One day with life and heart
Is more than time enough to find a world.
—James Russell Lowell

*T*he great cellist Pablo Casals once said, "For the past eighty years, I have started each day in the same manner. It is not a mechanical routine but something essential to my daily life. I go to the piano and I play two preludes and fugues of Bach. I cannot think of doing otherwise. It is a sort of benediction on the house. But that is not its only meaning for me. It is a rediscovery of the world in which I have the joy of being a part. It fills me with awareness of the wonder of life, with a feeling of the incredible marvel of being a human being."

What small thing can you do when you wake up in the morning to tap into that sense of marvel? Play a special piece of music? Read something inspirational? For me, it's cuddling in bed with my daughter, looking up at the redwood tree framed in the skylight, and listening to all the birds sing. We brew two cups of Earl Gray, dip our scones in them, and feel ourselves surrounded by nature.

45

"There is a subtle charm in the taste of tea which makes it irresistible and capable of idealisation. Western humourists were not slow to mingle the fragrance of their thought with its aroma. It has not the arrogance of wine, the self-consciousness of coffee, nor the simpering innocence of cocoa."
—Okakura Kakuzo, The Book of Tea

TEA

GOOD FOR WHAT AILS YOU

If you suffer from menstrual cramps or premenstrual discomfort, you may find the following bath remedy to be soothing and calming. The water will dilate your blood vessels and relax your muscles, while the herbs provide aromatherapy.

> 2 tablespoons dried lavender
> 2 tablespoons dried rose petals
> 3 tablespoons dried chamomile
> 2 tablespoons hops

Combine the herbs in a glass or ceramic bowl and pour in a quart of boiling water. Cover and let sit for an hour. Strain the herbs and pour under the running tap of a warm (not hot) bath.

*"The perfect temperature for tea
is two degrees hotter than just right."*
—Terri Guillemets

BASIL, MINT, AND ROSE HIP TEA

Some folks swear by hot tea in hot weather as a cool-down technique.

    12 ounces water
    2 tablespoons chopped fresh spearmint
    2 tablespoons chopped fresh basil
    2 rose hips teabags
    honey or sugar to taste (optional)

Place the water, spearmint, and basil in a nonreactive pan. Cover and bring the water to a rolling boil. Remove lid, stir, then add the teabags. Steep, covered, for 3 minutes. Strain tea into 2 warmed cups. Sweeten with honey or sugar, if desired. Serves 2.

RED VELVET CAKE

This cake is magnificent looking and tasting!

½ cup butter, margarine, or shortening
1 ½ cups sugar
2 eggs
1 teaspoon vanilla
3 tablespoons cocoa
2 ounces red food coloring
2 ½ cups sifted cake flour
1 cup buttermilk
1 teaspoon salt
1 teaspoon baking soda
1 tablespoon white vinegar

Preheat oven to 350°. Cream shortening and sugar until smooth. Add eggs and vanilla. Beat well. In a separate bowl, blend cocoa and food coloring; add to sugar mixture. Add flour, buttermilk, and salt alternatively. Mix soda and vinegar in cup and add to batter. Bake in two greased and floured 9-inch cake pans for 30 to 35 minutes or until a toothpick inserted in the center comes out clean. Let cool before frosting.

Polly, put the kettle on,
We'll all have tea.
—Polly, Put the Kettle On

The smell of new bread is comfortable
to the head and to the heart.
—Anonymous, circa 1400s

Here's a wonderful fall bread.

3 cups sugar	1 teaspoon baking powder
1 cup salad oil	1 teaspoon nutmeg
4 eggs, beaten	1 teaspoon allspice
1 16-ounce can pumpkin	1 teaspoon cinnamon
3 ½ cups sifted flour	½ teaspoon ground cloves
2 teaspoons baking soda	⅔ cup water
2 teaspoons salt	

Generously grease and flour two 9-by-5-inch loaf pans. Preheat oven to 350°. Cream sugar and oil in a large bowl. Add eggs and pumpkin; mix well. Sift together flour, baking soda, salt, baking powder, nutmeg, allspice, cinnamon, and cloves. Add to pumpkin mixture alternately with water. Mix well after each addition. Pour into two loaf pans. Bake for 1 ½ hours, until loaves test done. Let stand for 10 minutes. Remove from pans to cool. Makes 2 loaves.

CHRISTMAS TEA

Perfect for a post-tree trimming party, or on any winter's evening.

2 cups water, boiling
6 black tea bags
1 cinnamon stick
2 whole cloves
¼ cup sugar
2 cups cranberry/raspberry mix juice cocktail

Pour the boiling water over the tea bags and spices in a teapot. Cover and let steep for 5-6 minutes. In a medium-size saucepan, heat the juice until it's nearly boiling. Stir in the sugar. If your teapot is big enough, add the hot juice and serve from the teapot into fancy teacups.

Cookies

3 cups flour
½ teaspoon baking powder
⅛ teaspoon salt
1 cup butter or margarine
½ cup sugar
1 egg
2 teaspoons vanilla

Frosting

2 tablespoons hot water
1 cup confectioners' sugar
food coloring
chocolate sprinkles, cinnamon hearts, silver balls,
   red and green sugar sprinkles or other edible
   decorations

Preheat oven to 350°. Sift flour, baking powder, and salt in a medium bowl. In a large bowl, cream butter and sugar together. Add egg and vanilla and beat until fluffy. Gradually stir in sifted ingredients until well blended. Lightly flour a board. With a floured rolling pin, roll small amount of dough ⅛-inch thick. Cut with Christmas cookie cutters, such as trees, Santas, bells, etc. Bake on ungreased cookie sheets until brown, about 10–12 minutes. Place baked cookies on cooling rack. Repeat process until dough is gone.

While cookies are cooling, make the frosting. Combine the hot water and sugar in a medium bowl. Divide the frosting into thirds. Color one with green food coloring, one with red, and leave the third white.

When cookies are cool, decorate with the frosting and add the various sprinkles. Let your imagination go wild! Makes 5 dozen.

THE GIFT OF TEA

*W*hat better gift can you give someone than a little bit of relaxation and peace of mind in today's hectic world? Tea provides that perfect respite for almost anyone. You can find teapots and cute teacups just about anywhere—from a big department store to the boutique shop right around the corner. Tea's popularity makes it easy to find tea balls and infusers quite easily too. If you're in a big city, try your local Chinatown for new flavors to offer as a hostess gift, or subscribe a tea novice to a tea-of-the-month club—I found over fifteen online! A gift set from your local tea shop with some freshly-baked scones and cookies is the perfect housewarming treat for new neighbors. One more thing: don't forget to treat yourself! After a long day, put your tired feet up, take a little bit of time for yourself, and relax with a nice, steaming cup of comfort.

"Selection of afternoon tea food is entirely a matter of whim, and new food fads sweep through communities ... The present fad of a certain group in New York is bacon and toast sandwiches and fresh hot gingerbread. Let it be hoped for the sake of the small household that it will die out rather than become epidemic, since the gingerbread must be baked every afternoon, and the toast and bacon are two other items that come from a range."
—Emily Post, *Etiquette* (1922)

This old-fashioned gingerbread recipe dates back to colonial New England and is ideal for creating holiday "gingerbread people."

5 cups flour
3 cups sugar
1 ½ teaspoons baking soda
2 tablespoons ground ginger
1 pound butter, softened
3 eggs
1 ½ cups milk

Preheat oven to 375°. Sift together flour, sugar, baking soda, and ginger. Gradually combine with butter (mixture will feel coarse and crumbly). In a separate bowl, combine the eggs and milk, then add to the flour mixture, stirring until well blended. With a floured rolling pin, roll the dough out thinly onto a large baking sheet. With a cookie cutter, cut out shapes and place on a greased cookie sheet. Bake 5 to 10 minutes, or until brown.